The Bear Went Over the Mountain

The bear went over the mountain,

The bear went over the mountain,

The bear went over the mountain
To see what he could see.

The bear went through the forest,

4

The bear went through the forest,

The bear went through the forest
To see what he could see.

The bear went under the bridge,
The bear went under the bridge,

The bear went under the bridge,
To see what he could see.

The bear went into the cave,
The bear went into the cave,
The bear went into the cave . . .

And then he went to sleep!